An American Journey

An American Journey

The Photography of William England

Ian Jeffrey

Prestel

Munich · London · New York

Front jacket: New York from Trinity Church, looking towards the
bay and the New Jersey shore.
Frontispiece: "Along the tops" – The Victoria Bridge, Montreal.
The railway was fully enclosed, but later a twenty-inch wide slit was
cut the full length of the bridge to permit the emission of smoke.
Page 6: The Canadian Great Western Railway locomotive "Spitfire"
and tender.
Back jacket: General view of the American and Horseshoe Falls,
Niagara, from Prospect Point.

Acknowledgments
The author would like to thank Anne Armitage, librarian of the
American Museum in Bath, England.
Thanks also to Leon Meyer, Don O'Connor and Steve Eason at
Hulton Getty, and to Alicia Pau.

Editorial direction by Philippa Hurd

© Prestel Verlag, Munich · London · New York, 1999
© For the photographs by William England by Hulton Getty Picture
Collection, London, 1999

Library of Congress Catalog Card Number: 99-66060

Prestel Verlag, Mandlstraße 26, D-80802 Munich · Germany
Tel.: +49 (89) 381709-0; Fax: +49 (89) 381709-35

West 22nd Street, New York, NY 10010, USA
Tel.: (212) 627-8199; Fax (121) 627-9866

4 Bloomsbury Place, London WC1A 2QA
Tel.: (0171) 323 5004, Fax (0171) 636 8004

Prestel books are available worldwide.
Please contact your nearest bookseller or write to any
of the above addresses for information concerning
your local distributor.

Designed by Maja Thorn
Typesetting and lithography by LVD, Berlin
Printed and bound by Sellier, Freising
Paper: Galerie Art Silk 200 g/m² (Schneidersöhne)
Printed in Germany on acid-free paper

ISBN 3-7913-2158-7

Contents

Utopia 1859 *William England's America*

There have been many versions and visions of "America", some of them invented or contributed to by Europeans: the Wild West of the German writer Karl May, for instance, and the moody, delinquent USA of the 1950s and 1960s savored by such photographers as Robert Frank, a Swiss-American. By the 1950s there were any number of intersecting and overlapping versions of "America". But in the 1850s there seems to have been a more or less unitary idea of America as Arcadia, as a mountainous land of largely rural contentment ornamented by well-managed towns and cities of which New York was the chief exhibit. It was an idea of the United States which was irrevocably disturbed by the Civil War of 1861, and William England's composite picture—his American journey of 1859 recorded in stereo photography—ought to be seen as both the first large-scale photographic record of the country and the last glimpse of it as Utopia on a manageable scale.

A view in Sleepy Hollow, Tarrytown, New York.

The Stereo Background

Although of great importance in the history of photography, stereo has received relatively little attention in the principal accounts of the medium. In part this is because stereo cards are no more than a means to an end and not to be thought of as artworks in themselves. They are meant to be seen simultaneously through a twin-lens viewer, and to create an illusion of solidity, of substantial objects disposed in real space. Stereo illusions are often breathtaking, even if the subject itself is commonplace: idlers in the foreground, a bench overlooking a view, or a balustrade and a flight of steps. Stereo always supposed that we were open to its allures and that we were in some respects impressionable simpletons. Stereo might be taken, in other words, as belonging to another kind of history, perhaps to a history of entertainment. Photographic history has done itself a disservice in this respect because for many decades stereo was photography, from the 1850s right through to the Great War of 1914–18.

The term itself, *stereos*, was taken from the Greek for solid. Stereo photography had been under consideration almost from the beginning, from 1839 when photography was first announced in London and in Paris, by W.H. Fox Talbot and J.-L.-M. Daguerre. The stereo principle was developed in Britain by Sir Charles Wheatstone and realized by Sir David Brewster. The first functioning stereoscopic viewer was manufactured by the Parisian optician Jules Duboscq in 1850. In 1854 the London Stereoscopic Company was founded by George Swan Nottage, an entrepreneur from an ordinary background who went on to become Lord Mayor of London. Nottage employed William England who took these pictures of the northeastern United States and of southern Canada in 1859. By 1858, even before England had been to the United States, Nottage's company advertised a list of 100,000 different photographs of famous

Terrapin Tower and the pier from Goat Island, Niagara (stereo).

buildings and places of interest in Britain and overseas. Staff photographers such as England traveled far afield, although in the late 1850s they concentrated on urban subjects, Paris and New York in particular, both of which were cities in transition, subject to major building campaigns.

In New York stereo was developed by E. and H. T. Anthony during the 1850s. They had what they called an American and Foreign Stereoscopic Emporium at 501 Broadway. In addition to publishing and selling pictures they dealt in photographic materials, and continued to do so throughout the century. In France Adolphe Braun of Dornach was the first stereo magnate to emerge. Originally he had produced floral designs for the textile business. In the early 1850s the Anthonys had owned a portrait studio in New York. Stereo pointed to the existence of mass markets for photographic imagery, even though in the late 1850s no one quite knew what would be popular. This meant that early stereo entrepreneurs experimented with new and sometimes garish genres: sculpted novelty tableaux in one Parisian instance in which droves of skeletons acted all manner of social roles.

The first identifiable stereo genre to emerge was that of the Alpine Guide, a heroic male sombrely dressed at the head of a line of mountaineers in the Alps or the Pyrenees. Manufacturers and photographers continued to experiment, in particular with stereo transparencies. These were colored and pierced so that in certain controled lights it seemed as if the street lamps had just been lit, and the doors of taverns and shops opened to show the glowing hearths beyond. By the 1870s, however, stereo had begun to settle down, featuring more and more in an educational role, introducing the

English tourists trekking on the Chamonix Glacier, Switzerland, 1867.

world at large to home audiences. Certainly stereo became big business, and its later history is often told in terms of millions—of cards produced and viewers distributed. By the 1890s it was dominated by American companies: Underwood and Underwood, the Keystone View Company, and H. C. White & Co. Stereo companies were the first picture agencies too, providing material for the new illustrated periodicals and newspapers as these took shape during the first decade of the twentieth century. Stereo operatives reported on news as it happened, on the Boer War in South Africa and on the Russo-Japanese War of 1904. There are also comprehensive accounts in stereo of the Great War, but by then its attractions were being challenged by those of the cinema and the illustrated press. Stereo finally petered out in the 1920s, but only after it had done tremendous educational work. It was stereo which made audiences familiar with actualities worldwide, with the look of other places. Before the arrival of stereo the public had to make do with artists' interpreta-tions of mystifying and idealized landscapes from some romanticized Switzerland of the mind. Stereo, on the other hand, pointed out that else-where could be considered on a practical day-to-day basis as already familiar.

Touring in the USA

Stereo, in the hands of Nottage and the Anthonys, was a business, much like popular music would become in the twentieth century. Stocks of pic-tures were traded and companies were taken over and their libraries assimilated into new collections. Managers paid little attention to questions of authorship. It was sufficient that the image was of Niagara or of the Taj Mahal. Sometimes a photo-grapher was cited, but authorship seems to have meant relatively little in the stereo world. One of the remarkable things about this collection, on the other hand, is that it can be attributed to a single hand, that of William England, one of Nottage's principal photographers. It is also rare—indeed unique—in being a complete account of a

Interior of a sleeping car on the Canadian Great Western Railway.

single trip, through the Northeast. It was also, and as you would expect of a commer-cial photographer, a disciplined journey, one which took account of pictorial expecta-tions, for America, in particular, was a much traveled land and quite familiar to readers in Britain. Charles Dickens had toured in and reported on the USA in 1842, even if with a characteristic emphasis on prisons and on alms houses.

For those less preoccupied by social issues there was W.H. Bartlett's *American Scenery* of 1840. Bartlett had traveled in the northeastern corner of the United States in 1839 and 119 of his drawings were engraved and published by George Virtue in London, one of the leading publishers of the period. It is to *American Scenery* that England seems to have referred. Like Bartlett he took the view that it was in river scenery that America excelled, culminating in Niagara, the most celebrated natural phenomenon on earth.

River Scenery

England's is still to a large degree Bartlett's vision of America: New York as a thriving metropolis; Boston as a worthy provincial city; Niagara as the most sublime of specta-

Glen Ellis Falls, Pinkham Notch, in the White Mountains, New Hampshire.

cles, supported by any number of minor waterfalls in the Catskills, at Paterson, Trenton, and Rochester. Indeed England's confidence in the drawing power of waterfalls and cascades was unbounded: falling water from above and below, from both sides of the river, in the presence of bridges, with and without spectators. It would be tempting to explain this as no more than an aspect of contemporary taste. America was, in the words of Bartlett's writer N. P. Willis, the place for "river scenery", and there was a British appetite for such inculcated by exposure to the art of J.M.W. Turner and John Constable, and that of a whole range of watercolorists. All the same England's preoccupation with falling water is marked and deserves some attention.

In the High Romanticism of Constable and Turner the focus had been on rivers—on navigable rivers in Constable's case, with an emphasis on the uses of water, as signalled by tow-paths and lockgates. It is hard to attribute very specific values and meanings to their waterways, even though they do recall those of the Dutch seventeenth century when any torrent in a rocky landscape invoked both the Deluge and the possibility of Salvation. There were the Four Rivers of Paradise far in the background, and the baptismal River Jordan. But England, on business and traveling in comfort in sleeping cars on the newly established railroad system, gives the impression of a practical reporter to whom transcendental aesthetics would have been beside the point.

Even so, those cascades still draw attention to themselves. They recall many paintings of Gustave Courbet carried out more or less at the same time, from the mid-1850s through into the 1870s. These paintings, the most famous of which goes under the heading *Source of the Loue*, were made in numbers and in answer to popular demand, and are of rivers emerging from or near to their sources. Courbet's intention, as in much of his art, was to remark on the identity of a place, a region even, with respect to local rocks and stones and trees. Out of the many elements in a particular region a river source expresses identity most poignantly. If there is a point where a region can be said to begin it must surely be at the head of a river, for it is the river, as it enlarges, which characterizes the whole area. There is something of this identification of origins in England's pictures of modest cascades in the Catskills and in the White Mountains of New Hampshire. It was his way, as well as that of the culture at large, of locating the great metropolis in relation to native roots and to originating sites, some of which still carried Native American names. That is to say, the America England visited in 1859 could still be imagined in European terms, as a locality whose identity originated in local fea-

North view of Falls of the Passaic River at Paterson, New Jersey.

tures, rivers in particular. America was still, under these terms of reference, a natural rather than a political entity. Expansion of the railroads during the 1860s would relegate that ancient and organic vision of nationhood to history—and that more abstract future is also foretold in England's many photographs of trains, tracks, and depots.

There is, however, more to the cascade pictures than that. It must be remembered that they were meant to be seen in the stereo format, with all its emphasis on solidity. As illusions generated in stereo it would have been easy and tempting to imagine not just how the place looked but also how it sounded on the Passaic at Paterson or by the High Falls at Trenton. In romantic landscape earlier in the century sound was hardly a consideration to Constable and to Turner. The Thames flowed softly, without much fuss, through cultivated landscapes. Turner was more attentive to rough water on the Rhine, for example, but noise in his pictures is assimilated into light and vapor. The tendency then was to represent such spectacle visually, as if the eye were all-important and the chief agent of memory. In *American Scenery* in 1840 N.P. Willis described his experiences of Niagara several times, for Bartlett made seven drawings of it scattered throughout the book. It is as if hearing hardly came into the reckoning. Willis represented the Falls as a melodrama: "Suddenly the powerful stream is flung with accumulated swiftness among broken rocks; and, as you watch it from below, it seems tossed

The American Falls, Niagara.

with the first shock into the very sky. It descends in foam, and from this moment its agony commences. For three miles it tosses and resists, and, racked at every step by sharper rocks and increased rapidity, its unwilling and choked waves fly back, to be again precipitated onward, and at last reach the glossy curve, convulsed with supernatural horror." The Falls constituted a theatrical event: "As this misty curtain is withdrawn, the whole scene is disclosed." Travellers went there open to suggestion, knowing that the Falls would bring them as close to God as they were ever likely to be on the unsanctified surface of the Earth: "Niagara alone, of all the cataracts remains unchanged. He rolls on in his calm sublimity, spring and autumn, summer and winter, the same. His floods seem never to increase by the melting of snow, nor to be drunk up by the fervour of the sun. If changes he has, they are imperceptible, or seen only in the crumbling of rock beneath him, mountains at a convulsion, and at intervals of years." Dickens in 1842 was brought, if anything, even closer to the divine: "Then, when I felt how near to my Creator I was standing, the first effect, and the enduring one—instant and lasting—of the tremendous spectacle, was Peace. Peace of Mind, tranquillity, calm, recollections of the Dead, great thoughts of Eternal Rest and Happiness: nothing of gloom or terror. Niagara was at once stamped upon my heart, an Image of Beauty; to remain there, changeless and indelible, until its pulses cease to beat forever." Dickens was the most reverential of visitors, and outraged to find that in a visitors' book in a cottage on Table Rock, near to the Falls, that there were leaves "scrawled all over with the vilest and the filthiest ribaldry that ever human hogs delighted in."

Blondin's tightrope feat, crossing the Niagara River in the summer of 1859.

Funambulism

What happened between 1840 and 1859 was that humanity grew in confidence and boldness and took the Falls if not as an affront then as a challenge. Humanity's representative was Blondin, the French tightrope walker or "funambulist" as he was known. Blondin, born Jean François Gravelet, envisaged the crossing on a visit in the summer of 1858 and undertook the feat in 1859, although at a point a mile downstream from the Horseshoe Falls. Blondin, the Prince of Manila, made his crossing on a three-inch rope, two thousand feet long, at 160 feet above the surface of the river. He raised money through collection boxes to which the crowd contributed, and made the crossing time and again during the summer seasons of 1859 and 1860, once in a sack and once carrying someone on his back. He crossed pushing a wheelbarrow, and then dressed as a monkey. He carried a stove to the middle of the rope and cooked two omelettes, which he lowered on a rope to the boat *Maid of the Mist* waiting below. In 1860 a new funambulist appeared on the Niagara scene, a local man, William Leonard Hunt, alias Signor Guillermo Antonio Farini, also known as Farini the Great and Farini the Comical. The Falls, which had once been the source of sublime experience, became a backdrop for extraordinary stunts. The railways brought visitors in droves, and the hotel trade benefited enormously. Railway access was helped by the construction, between 1850 and 1855, of John Roebling's Niagara Suspension Bridge. This bridge, the first cable suspension bridge in the world to be used for rail traffic, appears in several of England's photographs. Indeed, Niagara's bridges seem to have interested him as much as the Falls themselves, which is quite understandable, for this was a great age of bridge building. Roebling's cables were an alternative to the tubular structures developed at the same time in England by Isambard Kingdom Brunel. British audiences would have been intrigued by the comparison.

Spectators watching Blondin's tightrope feat in the summer of 1859.

Interior of the Niagara Suspension Bridge.

The City's Streets

Discussion of Blondin, Farini the Great, and John Roebling does not, however, account for England's interest in falling water. To understand such particulars it is necessary to comprehend England's scheme as a whole. To some degree he was doing nothing new. His itinerary was substantially that of W. H. Bartlett twenty years before, and there was nothing original in the idea of an artistic tour; Turner carried out many such tours, and the results were engraved and published. The difference is that artists of Turner's generation thought in terms of the picture as an entity, complete in itself and centered on a view or building of interest, a priory, abbey, or castle. England, had he had the means at his disposal, might have composed as ambitiously, but stereo cameras delivered relatively small pictures of details and fragments of landscape. If a place was to be represented it had to be through a series of complementary views, so that an audience might build up a picture of New York City or of Niagara from however many images the stereo operative cared to provide.

View of Wall Street, New York, seen from Trinity Church (instantaneous photo).

17

Broadway, New York.

This meant that England was obliged to think of the series as an entity in itself, or as a large picture made up of a number of pieces, elements as it were in a mosaic. Thus all of the 234 pictures or so taken by England on his tour take their place within a wider context, and should be seen in relation to each other and as responses to other images in the set.

Now, one of the most intriguing aspects of early stereo, exemplified to perfection in these pictures, as its preoccupation with the city, with city streets in particular. All the great innovators in the late 1850s took pictures of major thoroughfares: the Anthonys and England in New York, George Washington Wilson in London and Edinburgh, and England and Adolphe Braun in Paris. The pictures look more or less the same: broad streets teeming with traffic and with pedestrians, taken from above, from a first floor balcony or from some significant viewpoint—England took pictures from Trinity Church in New York.

This was how the metropolis first emerged in photography. It is, however, necessary to be careful about these pictures, and not to see them simply as generalized crowd

*View of the Kaaterskill Glen,
Catskill Mountains, New York.*

scenes or even as rich in intriguing details. England, Braun, and the others placed
themselves to show their citizens less as individuals than as types of passers-by who,
at a certain distance in the picture, converge to form something approaching a stream
of human life, almost like a bloodstream, with the street or boulevard as a passageway.
Later generations might have come to think of the metropolis in terms of its major
buildings, but to these largely disregarded stereo artists of the late 1850s it was an organism constituted first and foremost of its inhabitants—business-like, swarming crea-
tures who took priority over the material fabric of the place. What is just as interesting
is that this was a vision of the city which did not survive, in photography at least.
Successors either concentrated on the buildings or the inhabitants, but never again on
the place as an organism or place of circulation. The metropolis to England and to his
contemporaries was, it appears, a fact of nature, to be considered under the same
aspect as natural phenomena, with respect, for instance, to all those streams in the
Catskills and in the White Mountains. The Falls at Trenton and Paterson were natural
and aural equivalents to Broadway busy with processions and passing traffic.

What exactly England's intentions were can never be known. Photography, from the very beginning, delivered a surplus of detail. There is one very good instance of this somewhat unsettling capacity on photography's part. England went to West Point, less because of its military associations than because of its reputation as a beauty spot. Willis, in his introduction to *American Scenery*, was in no doubt as to its attractions: "Of the river scenery of America, the Hudson, at West Point, is doubtless the boldest and most beautiful. ... Back from the bluff of West Point extends a natural platform of near half a mile square, high, level, and beautifully amphitheatred with wood and rock. This is the site of the Military Academy, and a splendid natural parade. When the tents of the summer camp are shining on the field—the flag, with its blood-bright stripes, waving against the foliage of the hills—the trumpet echoing from bluff to bluff, and the compact battalion cutting its trim line across the green-sward—there are few more fairy spots in this working-day world."

The ferry-boat to West Point from Garrison on the Hudson River, New York. The Military Academy is visible on the hill.

Bartlett, in his drawings of West Point, could give a sufficiently generalized and suggestive account of the place to support such an evocative description; but photography, by its very nature, was more practical in its appraisals. England must have traveled in the fall of the year, for although there are plenty of examples of trees in leaf in his series one of his scenes on the Hudson is entitled *Storing Wood for the Winter.* The image which immediately precedes it, number 32 in the reference series, shows a view of the river curving beautifully into the distance beyond a fenced foreground crossed by a line of five white sheds. Bartlett's account of the place shows that these were a mortar battery set to command the river. It looks, then, as if the white structures in England's view are covers meant to keep the mortars from damage by severe winter weather. No one at the time would have cared to remark on such marginal details, but it is on precisely this kind of evidence that photography has always insisted. Photography, especially in the documentary vein which England was practising long before the term had come into general use, depends on this sort of cryptic material, evidence awaiting a case in which it might testify.

"Storing wood for the winter."
Scene on the Hudson, New York.

The case at issue here involves when exactly the pictures were taken. It would appear, if those really are protective covers and if that stacked timber is a sign of approaching winter, that England traveled in the late summer and early fall of 1859. If that is so can he then have taken pictures of Blondin on his tight-rope over Niagara, because Blondin performed in the summer season when there were vacationing crowds to fill his collecting boxes. There is one picture of Blondin in England's set, and another of *Spectators watching Blondin's Tightrope Feat.* It is a possibility that he brought in his Blondin representation from a local operative; and likewise with his pictures of the Falls in winter conditions. Either the climate at Niagara was extraordinarily variable or he stayed there for a very long period, from summer into deep winter—all for the sake of a representative picture or two. Questions of authorship would hardly have troubled him, for he was there to take pictures for commercial distribution rather than to enhance his name. All this is to say that photography invited its audiences to behave forensically, as close readers of the evidence available; and that even when it wanted to it was unable to rise to the aesthetic heights so easily taken for granted by Bartlett and Willis—although not by Dickens who was greatly interested in the downside of his American experience: "smartness" verging, in his eyes, on criminality, and the misuse of tobacco in public places were two issues on which he felt strongly.

The Niagara Suspension Bridge. The entrance for foot passengers and horse carriages showing the rates of toll.

Deep Space, Bridges, and Railroads

England visited time-honored sites wherever possible. West Point and the Catskills were famous for good reason. He was, however, working with a relatively new medium with aesthetic premises of its own. Stereo gave a startling account of deep spaces of the kind which would have seemed quite uninteresting to Bartlett in the late 1830s. It was almost as if stereo had been devised to take account of new developments as they had occurred in the 1850s. The Hudson seen in a stereo viewer may have looked as impressive as ever it did in the 1830s but one of the new railroad lines or the road

The Niagara Suspension Bridge.
Interior of the carriageway.

through Roebling's new bridge at Niagara looked positively amazing. One of England's greatest pictures is of the Roebling bridge seen from the entrance. It was a two-tier affair with the railway on the upper deck and a lower level for carts and pedestrians. The stereo experience was almost that of a surveyor or even of a rifleman. It involved mastery of space, whereas the romantics thought rather of themselves as subject to space diffused. Perhaps stereo was no more than one manifestation of a new, more dominating turn of mind. In 1867, for instance, an Englishman, James Young, a chemical manufacturer from Widnes, traveled in the United States and kept a diary. On Saturday 7 September he traveled to Port Monmouth, thence by rail to Long Branch, "a distance altogether about 2 hours from New York." At Long Branch he stayed in the Continental Hotel where, in addition to quadrilles and other dances there was "a good billiard room, shooting gallery and nine-pin alley—the sport in the latter being enlivened by the presence of several young ladies who played with as much zeal as the gentlemen who accompanied them." Stereo ought to be thought of in the context of these entertainments, and as touching on skill rather than art.

England certainly appreciated this new spatial order, and took astounding pictures of the Niagara Suspension Bridge, inside and out, in section, and in profile. What precisely the bridge meant in the culture of the 1850s is open to question, but England hints at a meaning in one of his best photographs showing gatekeepers at the pedestrian level. The attendants sit at their ease by the entrance, with a lady pedestrian somewhere beyond, placed for the sake of scale. To the right England has included noticeboards giving details and regulations and tolls, clear enough to be read. What the new aesthetic did was to quantify space, to show it gauged in modular and calculable terms—and what might be gauged in that way could also be priced. That is, any landscape subject to railway culture was one which could be counted out financially or metered. The old order, characterized by "river scenery", was by contrast spontaneous and a reminder of a primordial state of affairs. To what degree England reflected self-consciously on this distinction cannot be known, but it is notable that his Arcadian landscapes, in the Catskills especially, sometimes show Nature in dangerous disorder characterized by tumbled rocks and shattered trees brought down in spring flooding.

Commercial Time

Humanity, too, was affected by this new order. In the old days, when Nature reigned, mankind stood by piously, lost in wonderment at the beauty and the spirit of the place;

and there are plenty of instances in England's pictures of that kind of stilled, respectful presence. The new time-kept and modular world made different kinds of demands. It was not part of God's bequest and therefore could not be reverenced. Yet people had to spend a great deal of time in its company, and the result was a new way of being in time. People waited in the new order; they waited for tolls to come their way, or they waited for the train to arrive—and there is one especially fine picture here, number 197 in the original series, of Clifton Depot, Great Western Railway, Canada.

Passengers waiting at the Clifton Depot, Canada. The Niagara Suspension Bridge is seen in the background.

Clifton Depot was within sight of a suspension bridge, whose pylons make the distance, and below the overhanging roof of the platform passengers and others await the arrival of the train. In this modern state of affairs you did business briskly, as on the teeming streets of New York, or you waited for the great mechanism to come your way. One

"Off to the Falls." The Maid of the Mist.

of England's most spectacular pictures, and one which ought to have been anthologized long ago, is of a solitary man seated on the cat-walk along the top of the enclosed Victoria Bridge at Montreal. He has been placed there to bear witness mainly, to give a sense of scale to the bridge stretching to infinity, and he sits as it were lost in thought rather than in wonderment (see frontispiece).

Less immediately striking but more interesting is a picture of the *Maid of the Mist*, the Niagara steamer which features in the exploits of Blondin and of Farini the Great, who once descended from his tightrope to drink champagne with its passengers. He photographed the *Maid of the Mist* at the riverbank, "off to the Falls", with the suspension bridge beyond. It was a paddle steamer, with one paddle to either side encased, and the cases served it seems as pedestals on which the crew could show themselves heroically. In 1857 George Washington Wilson had photographed a Thames steamer at Greenwich, featuring just such an heroic crewman scanning passengers on the quayside. England might even have had Wilson's picture in mind, but it would also be true to say that modern conditions as they were evolving in the 1850s staged humanity as never before. In the romantic era Nature was all-encompassing, if not all-important, but by 1859 what was of interest was the constructed or man-made environment. What could be more understandable than that those who held themselves responsible should want to appear to advantage on this new stage.

England opened his account with nineteen pictures of New York City, surprisingly few given its importance. By 1859, however, it was well documented by the Anthonys. He photographed from the top of the Brandreth Hotel, and from Trinity Church, making bird's-eye views of the kind which were commonplace in the 1850s and after. John Bachman's lithographs in particular virtually mapped the city, showing it almost in terms of lots and real estate, countable and calculable. England's is a similar prospectus of the city, with special attention to Broadway and to Wall Street. What is remarkable about his photographs of the city is that they make it look like almost anywhere else, much like Boston and like Montreal, despite New York's piquant reputation. Photography was no respecter of such reputations and saw one street full of buildings as being much like any other. Broadway especially had a great reputation for local color. It was noted above all, in the 1840s at least, for scavenging pigs. "Take care of the pigs," Dickens warned. "They are the city scavengers, these pigs. Ugly brutes

A group of Indian women at bead-work. Possibly taken on Goat Island, Niagara.

they are; having, for the most part, scanty brown backs, like the lids of old horsehair trunks: spotted with unwholesome black blotches. They have long, gaunt legs, too, and such peaked snouts, that if one of them could be persuaded to sit for his profile, nobody would recognise it for a pig's likeness. They are never attended upon, or fed, or driven, or caught, but are thrown upon their own resources in early life, and become preternaturally knowing in consequence." Broadway's scavenging pigs caught his imagination and won several paragraphs of his best prose. It was only in the 1890s, with the development of detective and panoramic cameras that the city's details would become available to photography. Until then they were part of the writer's province. Dickens also mentioned, after an account of Bowling Saloons off Broadway that the streets were unusually quiet: "Are there no itinerant bands; no wind or stringed instruments? No, not one. By day, are there no Punches, Fantoccini, Dancing-dogs, Jugglers, Conjurors, Orchestrinas, or even Barrel-organs? No, not one. Yes, I remember one. One barrel-organ and a dancing monkey—." England's New York City does seem busy enough with cabs and pedestrians, but there are relatively few types on show: a group of Indian women at bead-work under some trees in Canada, and another wayside scene in Canada, featuring a barrel-organ player with a monkey, and two attendants. England's is a remarkably sober account of America, sober because that is how America appears to have been in the 1850s.

It is hard to resist the idea that, Broadway's pigs apart, America in the 1850s and as rendered by William England epitomized order, or that it epitomized a kind of new Europe stripped of excrescences, "Punches, Fantoccini, Dancing-dogs" and the like. Commentators liked to remark on New York harbor, which appeared to exemplify efficiency. Willis compared it favorably with London: "The steam ferry-boats cross the half-mile between it (Brooklyn) and the city every five minutes; and in less time than it usually takes to thread the press of vehicles on London Bridge, the elegant equipages of the wealthy cross to Long Island for the afternoon drive; morning visits are interchanged between the residents in both places—and, indeed, the east river is hardly more of a separation than the same distance in a street." England took a fine picture of a ferry-boat in the bay of New York, and another of a boat and landing-stage with schooners in the background. These boats, far more than any of the city's buildings, stood for life in New York. James D. McCabe, Jr., described them in

"A Way-Side Scene, Canada."
Organ-grinders.

1872 in his *Lights and Shadows of New York Life; or, the Sights and Sensations of the Great City*: "The boats are generally handsome, as well as large. Nearly all are lighted with gas, and at least a score of them are to be seen in the stream at any time. At night, with their many coloured lamps, they give to the river quite a gala appearance. The Fulton, Barclay, and Cortlandt Street lines run their boats all night. The others run from 4 a.m. until midnight. The aggregate is said, by reliable authority, to be upwards of 200,000 persons per day, or about 75,000,000 per annum. Many of the boats carry from 800 to 1000 passengers at a single trip." McCabe discussed the ferries at length, analyzing patterns of traffic: working men at 5 a.m. succeeded by factory and shop girls, clerks and salesmen, clerks in the wholesale houses, and then "the great merchants themselves", followed by Wall Street men, great capitalists, idlers, and ladies. The industrious classes occupied themselves on the ferries by reading the daily papers, so that not a moment in the great movement of population was wasted.

England visited other cities: Washington, Philadelphia, Montreal, and Quebec. In Washington he photographed the White House, as well as the Capitol and the Treasury Building, both of which were still under construction. Washington was an unsuitable subject which made little impression on England. It was only recently developed, and lacked any traditional streets in the manner of Broadway. Thus, although there were high vantage points in Washington—such as the incomplete Capitol Building—they delivered disappointing prospects of scattered and widely spaced buildings. Philadelphia hardly seems to have interested him at all, apart from a view of sailing ships on the Delaware river and images of a horse-drawn streetcar and of the Saunders Monument, a marble statue of a woman with twins. Quebec likewise, "the Gibraltar of America", as Dickens described it, scarcely detained him. Dickens' account of Quebec is interesting with respect to England's neglect, for he saw Quebec in old, European terms: "Its giddy heights; its citadel suspended, as it were, in the air; its picturesque steep streets and frowning gateways; and the splendid views which burst upon the eye at every turn: it is at once unique and lasting." Quebec may have been pictorially exciting, but it was not typical nor expressive of the new America as a whole. Montreal seems to have attracted England far more, and Dickens' description of that city is again apposite: "The streets are generally narrow and irregular, as in most French towns of any age; but in the more modern parts of the city, they are wide and airy." It was modernity of this kind which answered to England's interest in orderly

View on the quay, New York.

perspectives which cut through the city. England's ideal was a teeming thoroughfare moving in a straight line from here to the horizon and overlooked by a high building on which he could set up his equipment. Boston has such a building in the shape of the State House. When Willis described Boston in the late 1830s it had been refurbished: "Alterations and additions have of late years greatly improved the appearance of Boston. The streets, which were formerly almost without exception narrow and crooked, have been in a great degree rendered wide and commodious; the old wooden structures have in the greater part of the city been replaced by handsome buildings of stone or brick. In the western part, particularly, there is much neatness and elegance. The splendour of the private buildings here, is not equalled in any other part of the Union." New York had had its own special high building in the shape of the Latting Observatory, an octagonal timber structure with iron supports. It had the first passenger elevator in the city and it faced 42nd Street, between Fifth and Sixth Avenues. It burned down in 1856, well ahead of England's arrival.

Water Power

There is one other important stopping point on England's itinerary: the Genessee Falls, on the Genessee, upriver from Rochester. There was a geological justification for looking at the Falls, for they were on the same escarpment as Niagara, but England seems to have been less interested in the spot because of its scenic beauty than for the sake of its installations. There was a notable High Bridge there, a trestle structure of six levels, made to carry a railway line; and the abundant waterpower in the area had been harnessed for industrial use—more conspicuously here than at any other place in America. It was a notable industrial site even in the late 1830s, when Willis had this to say of it: "At the Genessee Falls, as at Niagara, the descent to the lake is between the walls of a tremendous ravine, the grandeur of which seems to have had no terror for the souls of manufacturers. The thriving village of Rochester stands round the lip of the fall; and if you talk to the inhabitants of the beauty of the cascade, they stop your mouth, and strike calculation dumb, with the number of sledge-hammers, nail-cutters, mill-stones, and cotton-jennies, it carries; the product *per diem*—the only instance in the known world of a cataract turned, without the loss of a drop, through the pockets of speculators." England's expansive view of the Genesee river, with the High Bridge far in the background, looks like an attempt to do some justice to the entirety of the scene, although without citing specifically the sledge-hammers and other apparatus for which the place was renowned. It was as if he was content to acknowledge such elements, to hint at their existence, knowing perhaps that his audience was more amenable to Sleepy Hollow and its rustic bridge.

England took account of religion, even if cursorily, in the shape of an interior shot of Quebec Cathedral. History, too, was given short shrift, represented primarily by a statue of General Jackson on a prancing horse (Washington). He did, however, photograph George Washington's tomb, also, by the look of it, under construction. This is one of the most intriguing pictures in the series. It shows the brick façade and entrance

View of the Genesee River, near Rochester, New York.

to the tomb beyond duck-boards laid down by builders. An onlooker leans against the iron gate scrutinizing the tomb, and to the left stands a builder's ladder. It looks like the most casually contrived picture of a major monument, taken hastily and even in pass-

The tomb of Washington at Mount Vernon, Virginia.

ing. It testifies, if any picture ever did, to photography's commitment to unedited access to the present moment. This sort of candor would later become an article of faith in documentary photography, but in 1859 photography's constitution had still to be tabulated.

An Ideal Land

England's America is in the main circum-scribed and comfortable, everything in its place and Nature largely under control— with the exception of some of those storm-torn gorges in the Catskills and White Mountains. It was a vision of America which could not be sustained. The Civil War, which opened almost as England returned home, broke the mold, bring-ing news of terrible casualties and destruction. It also drew attention to other parts of the temporarily disunited States, to the classical and seigneurial South, and beyond that to the Frontier, which was represented in England's series only by a marble statue, *Incidents in the Life of a Pioneer*. The Civil War also served as a stimulus to photography. Matthew Brady, a successful portraitist in Washington, set up an organization to photo-graph the course of the war. A new generation of photographers came into being, many of whom went on to work for government organized surveys in the West and in California in particular. Henceforth there would be plenty of pictures of America, but the new photographers were specialists and regionalists, experts in mountain scenery and railway landscapes. The idea of a complete picture of the country and of its cul-ture passed into abeyance, only to be revived in the 1930s, in the form of Walker Evans's *American Photographs* of 1938. Robert Frank's *The Americans* (1958) also repre-sents the USA as a whole, but seen from a very particular outsider's point of view. Evans' USA was even more partial: a land of agriculturists and artisans contriving a hand-lettered, carpentered culture from primitive materials. England's by contrast, looks like a view of America by an insider, by someone who took it for granted that the USA was a unitary enterprise where everything was interesting without reservation. Cultural symbols—such as a ferry-boat or a Roebling bridge—meant the same thing to everyone in this apparently coherent culture. There were outsiders of a sort, such as the Canadian bead-makers and that little group of itinerants on the road's edge, but

Dickens himself had commented on the lack of serious long-term outsiders, punches, jugglers, and conjurors, and on the quietness of New York's streets, testament to the lack of other voices. England's America may, in fact, be the only surviving vision in the history of the medium of a society completely at one with itself. As events of the 1860s were to prove, this was a very false impression, but England seems to have had no intimation of what was about to happen. Yet as a representation of Utopia this picture of America ought to be honored, for it may be the only unselfconsciously realized vision of paradise on earth that we have.

Selected Bibliography

See Robert Taft's *Photography and the American Scene, a social history, 1839-1889*, first published by the Macmillan Company, New York, 1938. Although Taft makes no mention of England, who was a British photographer, he does refer to the Anthonys, whose stereo studies of New York precede those of England. They also distributed pictures of Blondin at Niagara.

William England is mentioned in Helmut and Alison Gernsheim's *The History of Photography, from the camera obscura to the beginning of the modern era*, first published by the Oxford University Press in 1955. They note that he invented the focal-plane shutter with variable slit, and that he described the working of this shutter to the Photographic Society of London in April 1862. To take his instantaneous street pictures he used this shutter with tannin dry plates. They also note that around 1866 he published an album of seventy-seven photographs entitled *Panoramic Views of Switzerland, Savoy. and Italy*, W. H. Bartlett's *American Scenery; or Land, Lake, and River Illustrations of Transatlantic Nature*, was published by George Virtue, London, in 1840, complete in thirty parts, each with four engravings and at least eight pages of historical and descriptive text.

Examples of Bartlett's imagery appear in Gloria Gilda Deák's *Picturing America 1497-1899: prints, maps, and drawings bearing on the new world discoveries and on the development of the territory that is now the United States*, published in two volumes by Princeton University Press, Princeton, NJ in 1988. Deák describes the visual culture which precedes England's visit. Charles Dickens' *American Notes* were first published in 1842. He provides one key to the understanding of England's pictures.

For an account of New York harbor in particular see James D. McCabe's *Lights and Shadows of New York Life; or, the Sights and Sensations of the Great City*, published by the National Publishing Company of Philadelphia, Cincinnati, Chicago, and St. Louis in 1872. For a history of Niagara Falls, with reference to its bridges, hotels, and funambulists, see Pierre Berton's *Niagara: A History of the Falls*, published in 1992 by McClelland & Stewart Inc., Toronto.

An artist at work in the Catskill Mountains, New York.

1859   *An American Journey*

New York from Trinity Church, looking towards the bay and the New Jersey Shore.

Wall Street, New York, from Trinity Church (instantaneous photo).

Whitehall Street and Bowling Green, from the Revenue Office, New York.

Barnum's American Museum of Curios, New York. Opened in 1841 on Broadway and Park Row, it was destroyed by fire in 1865.

Shops on Broadway, New York.

The military procession of the Atlantic Telegraph Jubilee, on Broadway, New York, to celebrate the laying of the transatlantic telegraph cable between the USA and Ireland.

Floating baths in the bay, New York.

Ferry-boats in the bay, New York.

Yonkers on the Hudson River, New York.

The High Bridge crossing the Harlem River, New York. Built as part of the Croton Aqueduct, it carried water to New York City.

Break-Neck Mountain at West Point, New York.

The ferry-boat to West Point from Garrison on the Hudson River, New York. The Military Academy is visible on the hill.

The Hudson River at West Point, New York.

West Point on the Hudson River, New York.

Rustic Bridge at Sleepy Hollow, Tarrytown, New York.

A small tunnel on the Hudson River railway, New York., which was opened in 1849.

"Indian Glen", Hudson River.

Natural Bridge, Virginia.

View of the Genesee River, near Rochester, New York.

The High Bridge over the Genesee River, near Rochester, New York.

The Columbia Railway Bridge over the Schuylkill River, near Philadelphia, Pennsylvania.

"Evening–A Rural Scene on the Schuylkill River", Pennsylvania.

"Crystal Cascade", Catskill Mountains, New York.

A cascade on the Kaaterskill River in the Catskill Mountains, New York.

The Fawn's Leap, Kaaterskill Clove, in the Catskill Mountains, New York.

View of the Kaaterskill Glen, Catskill Mountains, New York.

"Summer Recreations."

"A Quiet Evening", Sleepy Hollow, Tarrytown, New York.

The Flume, Franconia Notch, in the White Mountains, New Hampshire.

The Flume, Franconia Notch, in the White Mountains, New Hampshire.

A weir on the Schuylkill River in Philadelphia.

The Capitol, Washington D.C., under construction.

The Niagara Suspension Bridge—the upper railway deck. Completed in 1855 to carry the Grand Trunk Railway between Canada and New York State.

The Lewiston Suspension Bridge over the Niagara River. Built in 1851, it collapsed in a storm in 1864 because the stabilizing guy-wires has been disconnected to prevent the build-up of ice on the river below.

The rapids above the American Falls, and bridge to Goat Island, Niagara. Niagara Falls Village on the American shore can be seen left.

General view of the Niagara Falls, from Prospect Point.

The Niagara Suspension Bridge, seen from the landing-stage for the steamboat Maid of the Mist.

The Niagara Suspension Bridge, built to carry both rail and passenger traffic, with the Falls beyond.

The Terrapin Tower and Horseshoe Falls, Niagara, from Goat Island (instantaneous photo).
Built as an observation point in 1833 by Peter and Augustus Porter.

Panoramic view of the Horseshoe Falls, Niagara.

The "Cataract House" and rapids above the American Falls, Niagara, from Goat Island.

The Monteagle House, one of the many hotels built at Niagara.

Pastimes at the American and Horseshoe Falls, Niagara, from Prospect Point.

Prospect Point, Niagara. The booth advertising "Photographic and Stereoscopic Views of the Falls" belonged to Platt D. Babbitt.

"Winter Scene, Niagara."

Icebergs on the Niagara River.

The paddle-steamer ferry Maid of the Mist *on the Niagara River below the Falls.*
The second boat carrying the name, it was in service from July 1854 until late 1860 offering tours of the Falls.

The Spiral Staircase at Niagara, giving visitors access from Table Rock to a passage behind the Horseshoe Falls.

General view of Montreal.

Montreal from Nôtre Dame basilica.

Shipbuilding on the St. Lawrence River at Quebec.

The St. Lawrence River looking towards the Victoria Bridge, Montreal.

The Haut-Ville or Upper Town and the Citadel of Quebec, from Point Levi.

The riverboat Salaberry on the Lachine Canal, Montreal.

The entrance to the Victoria Bridge over the St. Lawrence River, Montreal.

The Victoria Bridge, Montreal. The single-track railway bridge, built to an enclosed tubular design, was opened by Edward, Prince of Wales in August 1860.

The Victoria Bridge, Montreal, from the shore of the St. Lawrence River.

The Canadian Great Western Railway locomotive "Essex", at Clifton Depot.

View on the Montmorenci River, Quebec.

The Chaudière Falls on the Ontario River.

William England, his Times and Contemporaries

William England and his Times

Biography of William England*

Photographic and Art History*

1854–62 England joins the London Stereoscopic Co., becoming its chief photographer and contributing to its reputation with thousands of plates of stereoscopic views.

1830 William England is born in London, England.

1840–45 He works in a daguerreotype studio in London.

1854 England abandons portraiture.

1854–62 England joins the London Stereoscopic Co., becoming its chief photographer and contributing to its reputation with thousands of plates of stereoscopic views.

He invents and pioneers the "focal-plane shutter" camera which greatly improved clarity, revolutionizing the art of photography.

1825 **Thomas Cole**, America's leading landscape painter, makes a sketching tour of the Hudson River and up onto the Catskill Mountains near New York.

1826 **William Henry Fox Talbot**, contributor to the invention of photography, begins experimenting with photogenic drawings in England.

1837 **Louis Jacques Mandé Daguerre**, one of the most famous French inventors of photography, creates his first daguerreotype in France.

1838 **Sir Charles Wheatstone**, scientist at Kings College London, gives an address to Royal Society of Arts, London on the phenomenon of binocular vision and proposes the equipment be called a Stereoscope.

1839 Photography is first announced in Paris then London by **J. L. M. Daguerre**. and **W. H. Fox Talbot** respectively.
The daguerreotype is publicly announced at the Academy of Sciences Paris. The first commercially manufactured daguerreotype camera named Giroux is introduced.
Alexander Wolcott receives first American patent in photography for his camera.
The Petzval lens is introduced which is 16 times faster than others at the time.
British landscape artist, **W. H. Bartlett** travels to the northeastern corner of America, his sketches are in *American Scenery*, 2 vols., published by George Virtue, London 1840.

1840 Stereo principle is developed by **Sir Charles Wheatstone** in England.

1858	He travels to Ireland.	1841	Charles Dickens tours the USA. The resulting work, *American Notes*, was published in 1842.

1858   He travels to Ireland.

1859   England goes to the USA, and produces the series *America*, the first photos of the United States distributed in Europe commercially. His pictures show a train crossing the Niagara River, Blondin crossing the Niagara Falls on his tightrope (the company's best-selling image of all time), and many landscapes.

1861   He visits Paris.
England invents a shutter of variable openings, the forerunner of the modern single lens reflex camera.

1862   He photographs the International Exhibition in London.

1863   England concentrates on freelance work. He produces a series on Switzerland. He uses a camera with two lenses (divergence of 8 or 9 cm). He takes care to compose his subject always with the first planes quite removed from the main scene.

1863–65 England publishes stereoscopic views taken during the summer in Switzerland, the Tyrol, and Italy. As a specialist in Alpine views, he has the patronage and support of the British Alpine Club who publish some of his images.

1865   He publishes an album containing 77 panoramic views of Switzerland, Savoy, and Italy.

1841   Charles Dickens tours the USA. The resulting work, *American Notes*, was published in 1842.

1850   Two American photo journals begin, the *Daguerreian Art Journal* and the *Photographic Art Journal*.
A functioning stereoscopic viewer is manufactured by optician Jules Duboscq.
E. and H. T. Anthony develop stereo at the American and Foreign Stereoscopic Emporium on Broadway.
Mathew Brady publishes a collection entitled *A Gallery of Illustrious Americans.*

1851   Daguerreotypes are exhibited at the Great Exhibition of the Industry of All Nations held at London's Crystal Palace.

1853   **Platt D. Babbitt**, opens a daguerreotype studio in Niagara Falls. He chooses Horseshoe Falls as the backdrop for his group portraits.

1854   George Swan Nottage founds the London Stereoscopic Company.

1855   John Roebling's (also the architect for the Brooklyn Bridge) Niagara Suspension Bridge is completed.

1856   **William Notman** settles in Montreal and commences stereoscopic work the same year as England's visit.

1857   **Frederick Edwin Church** uses daguerreotypes and photographs to construct his "heroic landscape" of Niagara (the representation is topologically impossible even though it looked real). It is exhibited in London and New York in 1858 and 1859. The Great Western Railway runs its first sleeping-car for passengers.

1858   **William and Frederick Langenheim** publish *American Stereographic Views.*

1859   French tightrope walker, Blondin (born Jean François Gravelet), crosses downstream from the Horseshoe Falls, Niagara.
Sutton panoramic camera is patented.

1866   England erects a studio in Notting Hill, London, for portraiture and printing from landscape negatives.

1867   He publishes an album of 72 panoramic views of the Rhine.

1871   England is made a member of the London Photographic Society. He sends a note about cracks appearing in the collodion layer on plates: his remedy is polishing.

1886   England becomes vice-president of the London Photographic Society. He is made president the same year.

1887   He presents photolithograhs and copies of etchings at the Crystal Palace, London.
        He begins to use gelatine chloride plates.

1889   England is one of the judges at the Universal Exhibition and later becomes vice-president of the jury.
        He is made a chairman of the West London Photographic Society of which he is a member.

1890   England runs the Solar Club (GB).

1896   William England dies in London.

1859–63 **Oliver Wendell Holmes**, American essayist, writes three articles for the *Atlantic Monthly* describing photography as an empowering and all-encompassing instrument of modern life.

1859   Expansion of the railroads.
        Mathew Brady photographs Abraham Lincoln during his first presidential campaign.

1860   Edward, Prince of Wales, tours North America and opens Victoria Bridge, Montreal.
        Oliver Wendell Holmes invents a popular stereoscope viewer.

1861–65 US Civil War—documented by **Mathew Brady**.

1870s   Pioneering landscape photography of the American West begins with Timothy O'Sullivan. Other notable landscape photographers include William Henry Jackson and Carleton Watkins.

1870s   Stereo becomes more of an educational tool.

1870   America dominates the stereo market; Underwood & Underwood, The Keystone View Company, H. C. White and Co. Stereo.

1893   The Stereoscopic Society is founded, and is one of the two societies operating in Britain which continue to promote this form of photography.

Contemporaries of William England

ANTHONY, Edward   b. 1818; d. 1888
ANTHONY, Henry T.   b. 1814; d. 1884

Edward Anthony learnt the daguerrotype process from Samuel F. B. Morse. His first major photographic venture was on an expedition to the borders of the eastern USA and Canada. The E. and T. H. Anthony Company, producing views and *cartes de visite*, started in 1850, although Edward had been importing and supplying daguerrotype materials and chemicals to photographers such as Mathew Brady since 1847. Edward Anthony himself took "instantaneous" stereographs of people and street scenes in New York. In 1907 the business merged to become the Ansco Company, later renamed Agfa.

BABBITT, Platt D.   d. 1879

In the mid-1850s Platt D. Babbitt produced whole-plate daguerreotypes for his group portraits on the American side of the Niagara Falls. This gave tourists an image of their trip to display at home or to enjoy through the magic of the Grand Parlor Stereoscope. By 1855 Babbitt had set up such a machine in a local Niagara hotel, acquiring the equipment from Southworth and Hawes. Tourists were thus able to compare the real suspension bridges outside with the three-dimensional stereographic reproductions viewable in the hotel lobby. Having a monopoly of photography at Prospect Point, Babbitt's booth is visible in William England's view shown on page 79.

BARTLETT, William Henry   b. 1809, d. 1854
William Henry Bartlett was famous for his views of all

parts of the world. He traveled several times to America where he gathered sketches for his book *American Scenery*. This was a collection of natural wonders, city landmarks, and architectural monuments. It was one of the most popular series of its kind in the nineteenth century. The series was first issued in parts from June 1837 to November 1839; it then became two volumes of a book in January 1840. Bartlett's prints of Niagara Falls are among his most famous and represent what a typical tourist would have seen during a visit to the Falls.

BRADY, Mathew   b. 1823; d. 15 January 1896

Mathew Brady began his photographic studies with Samuel F. B. Morse. In 1839 he met Louis Daguerre after which he set up a successful gallery in the USA capitalizing on the success of the daguerreotype. Brady began to photograph famous people such as Abraham Lincoln during Lincoln's first presidential campaign of 1859. *A Gallery of Illustrious Americans* published in 1850 made his portraits more widely known.

Between 1844 and 1858 Brady set up numerous gallery-studios which were described thus in the *New York Illustrated News*: "M. B. Brady, Esq., the eminent daguerreotypist, has lately opened a new saloon for the purposes of his art, in one of the best buildings on Broadway, New York. On the occasion of the first opening, a large number of ladies and gentlemen, comprising many distinguished persons, were invited, and partook of Brady's hospitality at a splendid dinner. The salon is one hundred and fifty feet long, finished and furnished in the most costly manner."
On 26 March 1851 the newspaper also remarked: "Mr. Brady is one of the oldest daguerreotype artists in

the country, and one of the most successful, too. He is the author of many valuable improvements connected with the art, his pictures having a world-wide fame for fidelity and elegance."

Brady employed a team of photographers to work with him when documenting the American Civil War (1861–65). He was a pioneer of real documentary photography who did not rely on posed shots. He claimed that "the camera is the eye of history", however his photographs were too graphic for public acceptance. The *New York Times* wrote on 20 October 1862: "Mr. Brady has done something to bring home to us the terrible reality and earnestness of war. If he has not brought and laid them on our door-yards and along the streets, he has done something very like it...." Most of Brady's collection is located in the House of Congress, Washington.

CHURCH, Frederick Edwin
b. 4 May 1826; d. 7 April 1900

Frederick Edwin Church was born in Hartford, Connecticut. Against his father's wishes he studied with a local landscape and portrait painter, Alexander H. Emmons (1816–1879) in Hertford. In 1844 Church was the first pupil to be taken on by Thomas Cole. His debut was at the annual exhibition of the National Academy of Design in New York and by 1849 he was the youngest person elected (age 23) to full membership in the National Academy. During the 1840s and 1850s Church travelled widely in South America and became more ambitious in his painting. When he exhibited his paintings of Niagara (composed using daguerreotypes) in New York and London in 1858 and 1859 his reputation was established as America's most prominent landscape painter.

COLE, Thomas
b. 1 February 1801; d. 11 February 1848

Born in Lancashire, at the age of 14 Cole became assistant to an engraver and apprentice to a designer of calico prints. In 1819 he joined his parents in Ohio where he later learned to paint. In 1825 he moved to New York and that summer made numerous sketches of the Catskills and the Hudson River. William England used the same rural motifs that Cole depicted in his paintings, including the pictorial device of figures sketching and climbing the Falls, as seen in the views shown on pages 33, 58, 59, and 60.

In 1829 Cole travelled to England where he met painters J. M. W. Turner (1775–1851) and John Constable (1776–1837). In 1836 he returned to the Catskills where he married. In 1844 Frederick Edwin Church became his pupil and continued in Cole's footsteps, painting American landscapes with more accuracy and attention to light and atmosphere. Cole became known as America's leading landscape painter during the early nineteenth century and his influence was reflected in many younger artists and landscape photographers who matured in the 1850s.

DAGUERRE, Louis Jacques Mandé
b. 18 November 1787; d. 10 July 1851

In 1803 Daguerre began work in a Paris theater. He was well known for his illusionistic form of theater called the diorama. As a device to help in painting stage sets, he used a camera obscura which led him to focus on freezing the image.

In 1835, after working with Nicéphore Niépce for four years, Daguerre made an important discovery by accident. He left an exposed plate in a cupboard with a broken thermometer, and after a few days he found that the latent image had developed. Daguerre concluded that this was due to the presence of mercury vapor. On 19 August, after the French government bought the rights to the process from him, the process was announced publicly. Only five days before, this process, now known as the daguerrotype, had been patented in England.

The *Literary Gazette* of 7 January 1839 wrote: "We have much pleasure in announcing an important discovery made by M. Daguerre, the celebrated painter of the Diorama. This discovery seems like a prodigy. It disconcerts all the theories of science in light and optics and, if borne out, promises to make a revolution in the arts of design. M. Daguerre has discovered a method to fix the images which are represented at the back of a camera obscura, so that these images are not the temporary reflection of the object, but their fixed and durable impress, which may be removed from the presence of those objects like a picture or an engraving."

Daguerre died in 1851. That same year the wet-collodion process was invented by Frederick Scott Archer, announcing the beginning of a new era in photography. The discovery was not welcomed in all quarters, however, and many artists were concerned that the daguerreotype would mean the death of painting. In 1859 French poet Charles Baudelaire wrote: "If it [photography] is allowed to encroach upon the domain of the … imaginary, upon anything whose value depends solely upon the addition of something of a man's soul, then it will be so much the worse for us."

HOLMES, Oliver Wendell   b. 1809

Oliver Wendell Holmes was born in Cambridge, Massachusetts. He graduated at Harvard in 1829 in medicine and completed his studies in 1836. He held the chair of anatomy and physiology in Dartmouth until 1847, and then at Harvard.

Holmes is best known as a popular American writer who was a poet, physician, and humorist. He wrote in the *Atlantic Monthly* between 1859 and 1863, describing the power of photography: "Surfaces look solid … as to produce the appearance of reality which cheat[ed] the senses with its seeming truth.… Dream-like

exaltation, in which [the viewers] seem[ed] to leave the body behind and sail away into one strange scene after another, like disembodied spirits. …a surprise such as no painting ever produced."

LANGENHEIM, William   b. 1807; d. 1874
LANGENHEIM, Frederick   b. 1809; d. 1879

The Langenheim brothers were born in Germany. As photographers they worked in Philadelphia, producing a series of forty daguerrotypes of the Niagara Falls in 1845. In 1848 they paid Fox Talbot $6000 for the US patent rights to the calotype process. The venture did not pay off, however, as the calotype was not popular in the USA, and it was only later with the development of the wet-collodion process that the brothers saw success with stereoscopic views, in particular their 1854–56 series which was published in 1858 as *American Stereographic Views*. Their American Stereographic Co. was sold to E. and H. T. Anthony in 1861.

NOTMAN, William   b. 1826, d. 1891

Scottish-born William Notman moved to Canada in 1856. He began producing stereoscopic views of Niagara in 1859, the same year as England's visit. He became known for large-plate views of Canadian scenery and Niagara Falls in particular. Appointed photographer to Queen Victoria in 1861 after his recording of her son's visit to Montreal the previous year his fame grew with the publication in 1863 of *Notman's Photographic Selections*, the first of two volumes. Alongside his work as a photographer of outdoor scenes, Notman maintained a successful portrait photography business in Montreal.

TALBOT, William Henry Fox
b. 11 February 1800; d. 17 September 1877

Fox Talbot studied classics and mathematics at Cambridge University, England. In 1822 he became a fellow of the Royal Astronomical Society and a fellow of the Royal Society of London in 1832. He was also a Botanist, an MP, and Assyriologist.

On 25 January 1839 he announced the discovery of a method of "photogenic drawing" at the Royal Institute. By chance, in September 1840, whilst trying to re-sensitize paper Fox Talbot discovered the phenome-non of the latent image. This dramatically lowered exposure times—from one hour or so to between one and three minutes. Fox Talbot called the improved version the calotype.

On 31 January 1841 Fox Talbot gave a paper to the Royal Society of London entitled "Some account of the Art of Photogenic drawing, or the process by which natural objects may be made to delineate them-selves without the aid of the artist's pencil." Talbot patented his invention in 1841, however calotypes never became popular partly due to the restrictions of the patent (as the Langenheim brothers discovered) and partly because they were inferior to daguerreo-types in their reproduction of detail.

In 1844 Talbot produced the first commercial book illustrated with photographs, titled *The Pencil of Nature*. The Royal Photographic Society in Bath, England, has two complete sets of the limited edition of *The Pencil of Nature*, together with many of Fox Talbot's letters, books, and documents.

The earliest surviving paper negative, dated August 1835, of the Oriel window is in the South Gallery at Lacock Abbey, Wiltshire, England, where Talbot lived.

WHEATSTONE, Sir Charles
b. 6 February 1802; d. 19 October 1875

Wheatstone became Professor of Experimental Philosophy at Kings College, London. Although known as a physicist who contributed to the invention of telegraphy, in the history of photography he is known for his work in aiding the development of stereoscopy.

In June 1838, at the Royal Scottish Society of Arts,

Wheatstone introduced his theory of the phenomena of binocular vision. He said: "I … propose that it be called a Stereoscope, to indicate its property of repre-senting solid figures." He then presented his stereo-scope which is preserved in the Science Museum in London, England. The stereoscope was extremely popular during the exhibition at Crystal Palace, London in 1851 where Queen Victoria and Prince Albert both experienced the representation of "solid figures". Following this, a huge trade developed in stereoscopic daguerreotypes and images.

Wheatstone's mirror stereoscopic viewer had the advantage that it could cope with large pictures. Today, the same principle is used in X-ray stereoscopic pictures.

The commercial photographer, Jean François Antoine Claudet (1797–1867) who became fascinated by the stereoscopic daguerreotypes wrote: "The stereoscope is the general panorama of the world. It brings in the cheapest and most portable form, not only the picture but also the model, in a tangible shape, of all that exists in the world in various countries of the globe. … We have the advantage of examining (the pictures) without being exposed to the fatigue … and risks of the daring and enterprising artists who, for our gratification and instruction, have traversed lands and seas, crossed valleys, ascended rocks and mountains with their heavy photographic baggage…."

WOLCOTT, Alexander   b. 1804; d. 1844

Wolcott was an American daguerreotype photo-grapher and instrument maker. He invented a camera which had a large concave mirror that reflected light on to the plate. Although the plate was only 5cm^2 it greatly shortened exposure time and meant the image was no longer laterally reversed. Wolcott opened the world's first portrait studio in March 1840.